Selling Commodity Options
The Time Farming Income Machine

BY DON A. SINGLETARY

There is no substitute for a good reference book of strategies, definitions, and trading ideas like those found in this book. Every modern option trader using fast on-line fills and low commission rates - has to learn to rely on himself if he or she wishes to trade with the confidence it takes to make money consistently.

This publication is intended to provide training information and commentary on the subjects covered. It is sold with the understanding that neither the author nor the publisher is engaged in rendering legal, accounting, securities trading, or other professional services. If legal advice or other expert assistance is required, the services of a competent professional person should be sought. Any trades, observations, and opinions based on real or fictitious equities, are used for illustration and teaching purposes only in this book- and are not intended to be trading advice on any specific equities or products. The trades, strategies, and products in this book have risks and using them can and does result in losses.

Foreword

By: Michael Gross

I first met Don Singletary after reading his *Options Exposed Playbook*.

As a professional portfolio manager, I have read literally hundreds of books on options and trading over the course of my career. Of those, I could pick about a dozen that are actually worth more than the paper they are printed on.

Don's first book on Options trading was one of those. As a former commodities hedge consultant, Don brings an interesting, highly valuable (and potentially profitable) perspective to the subject of options trading.

But it was his down to earth, "cut to the chase" explanations that really pulled me into his book. Don has a gift for making the complex simple. His entertaining and instructive use of metaphor is one of his greatest gifts – one that any option trader can be thankful for.

After reading the Options Exposed Playbook, I contacted Don to see if he would be willing to do an interview for our monthly newsletter. Don agreed and I was fascinated by his straight forward and original answers. In a world where many publish simply to publish, Don is an author and teacher that truly has something to say. He brings his lessons in options trading from personal experience – not from complex theories he read in a reference manual or pulled from a computer data screen.

In short, he's the real deal. I recommend Don's work to any aspiring option trader or even experienced professional. Whether beginner or seasoned pro – there is something you can gain from his insights.

When I found out Don was writing a book on selling commodities options, I jumped at the opportunity to write the forward – and was honored Don had considered me.

Having some experience in this field myself, I was eager to see what Don had put together. As expected, I was not disappointed.

Commodities option selling is a little-known corner of the investment world – yet one that can offer some unique and lucrative benefits – especially for individual investors.

Knowing how to approach this form of investing, however, is paramount. This new work shows you how to do exactly that and more, all presented in Don's characteristic informative yet entertaining style.

I am proud to call Don a colleague and friend and have no doubt that his works will one day be considered investment classics. *Selling Commodity Options The Time Farming Income Machine* will, in my opinion, be near the top of that list.

Learn, digest and apply this strategy and you'll be well on your way to targeting high yields and income in any type of market environment or economy. And you'll be doing it with an approach that few investors have ever heard of.

Happy option selling!

Michael Gross, *Director of Research-OptionSellers.com, Co-Author of McGraw-Hill's The Complete Guide to Option Selling*

Just because the market is open does not mean you have to trade.
Cash is a position too.

Control your own destiny or someone else will.

Any trader can take risk, a great trader can do it with purpose and use it to their advantage. – the author

Order your free bonus chapter for this book now. Just send me an email to Don@WriteThisDown.com and put TIME FARMING in the subject line to receive the free PDF file. This includes important resource links for research, tips on selecting trades, help with which strikes to use, and suggestions for money management when time farming.

Table of Contents

Introduction

You are about to be introduced to a very specific strategy that few personal investors have even heard of. It's a strategy that professional investors use every day and now the time has come, due to new technology and modern trading platforms, to introduce it on a larger scale as a practical strategy for many personal investors. The strategies in this book identify certain commodity options that have around a 90% or more chance of expiring worthless and illustrate how you can sell them and pocket the profit. About 80% of all options expire worthless, and selling *selected* options is the key to an even higher probability of success.

- Learn to use a trading and option strategy that will allow you to trade with virtually the same odds that insurance companies and casinos use to make money consistently.
- This method is entirely independent of the stock market; no matter if stocks are up, down, or neutral, these strategies work year round.
- Many commodity seasonal trends (price patterns) are determined by nature. Trading in harmony with these seasonal trends can be like sailing with the wind at your back.

For over twenty-five years, I was a private consultant to major corporations in commodity hedge risk management. I have more than 20,000 hours of experience as a professional in the field of commodity ag options. My clients used strategies incorporating commodity options to mitigate risks and lock in acceptable margins.

The goal is to show you how to trade smart and control risks by keeping the odds highly in your favor, just like the pros do. This is a book about high probability trades. More specifically, you'll learn how to find options on commodities that are extremely likely to expire worthless. Selected option trades are very far out-of-the-money and they use time-decay in conjunction with smart option strategies, principles as dependable as gravity. You'll learn how to identify and sell them to get a cash credit in your account. I have coined the phrase **Time Farming**® to describe this process.

There are new opportunities for personal investors that just were not available until recently. Most ag commodity options weren't introduced until 1989. Since then, technical innovations have roared through the markets: fast inexpensive computers, powerful free software, lightning fast network data, and deeply discounted commissions. These innovations have leveled the playing field between professional and personal investors. This type of investing is not for everyone. There are those rare points in time, when a real game-changing strategy is available to the personal investor. This is one of those times, and this book is your gateway to this unique strategy.

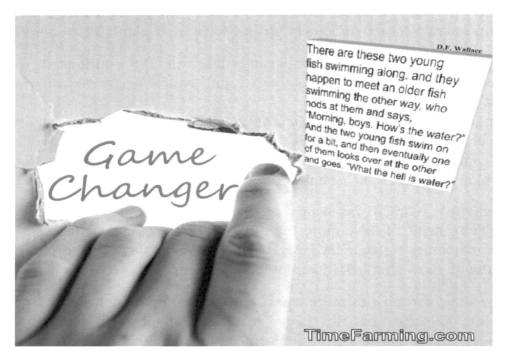

- **The way to risk going broke is to buy options and try to guess price moves over short periods of time.**
- **The way to make money is to be an option seller, and place trades that do not depend on correctly guessing price movements or exact timing.**

Chapter 1
The Power of Mother Nature

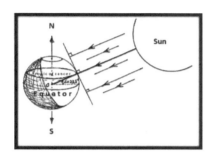
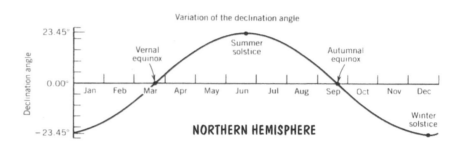

How would you like to take a trip to the bank while holding hands with Mother Nature?

Informed traders like predictability – and the seasons of Earth provide it. People use more heating oil in winter, more gasoline in the summer, and most crops will be planted in spring and harvested in the autumn. The commodities markets operate independently of the stock market and often provide many attractive alternative investments. *Time Farming* is all about being aware of seasonal price tendencies in the commodity markets.

Unlike the stock market, where each investment represents a share of a company or venture, the commodity markets buy and sell *contracts* to deliver a set amount of an underlying physical commodity. One contract of corn represents 5,000 bushels and the price is quoted in cents per bushel. Each futures contract promises delivery of a commodity in a specific month. Corn, like other commodity futures contracts, trade in *contract months* that are named for the delivery date of the contract. The illustration that follows this paragraph is a part of the *contract spec sheet* from CME (Chicago Merc Exchange). A nearby contract is the next (the nearest in date) that will expire. Conversely, a *distant contract* is a contract that expires *further out in time*.

Corn Futures

The designated contracts for corn (see "listed contracts" in the table) are MAR, MAY, JUL, SEP, and DEC. Contract symbols (corn = ZC) use a one letter month designation followed by a one-digit number for the year of the contract. For example, the JUL 2018 contract for corn uses this symbol: ZCN8 (ZC = corn) All futures contracts uniformly use these one-letter symbols for the months.

MONTH SYMBOLS

JAN = F	JUL = N
FEB = G	AUG = Q
MAR = H	SEP = U
APR = J	OCT = V
MAY = K	NOV = X
JUN = M	DEC = Z

CORN CONTRACT SPECIFICATIONS

Contract Unit	5,000 bushels (~ 127 Metric Tons)
Price Quotation	Cents per bushel
Trading Hours	Sunday – Friday, 7:00 p.m. – 7:45 a.m. CT and Monday – Friday, 8:30 a.m. – 1:20 p.m. CT
Minimum Price Fluctuation	1/4 of one cent per bushel ($12.50 per contract)
Product Code	CME Globex: ZC CME ClearPort: C Clearing: C TAS: ZCT
Listed Contracts	March (H), May (K), July (N), September (U) & December (Z)
Settlement Method	Deliverable
Termination Of Trading	The business day prior to the 15th calendar day of the contract month

(SOURCE: CMEGROUP.COM this is a partial page)

FREE EDUCATION

Free Basic Futures Education

The CME has an excellent basic course on futures and commodity trading and it is all FREE for you. It has professionally produced videos and texts to teach you the basics. The nice thing about CME course(s) at this site is that it is commercial free and unbiased material, no annoying sales pitches of any kind – and the quality is superb. The business of this book is to show you how to find trades and understand how they work. The basic CME course will teach you about futures, terms, and to grasp why these markets exist and are so vitally important. If you just need a review, then you are able to skip over any section(s) at will. You will need to know this material in order to understand the trades and illustrations in this book. Our thanks to CME.

CME BASIC FUTURES COURSE: http://futuresfundamentals.cmegroup.com

CMA COURSE CATALOG: http://institute.cmegroup.com/learn/course-catalog

Corn Seasonal Prices DEC Futures Contract

"The Grains" category of futures contracts usually includes: corn, wheat, oats, and soy beans, even though technically soy is an oil seed. This group has some of the most predictable price patterns, although you should be aware that there are often counter-seasonal price trends years due to occurrences such as drought, floods, disease, supply-demand, trade agreements, and other factors. This *grains group trade* in 5000 bushel contracts, and on the same days and times.

Remember corn trades in named contract months of H, K, N, and Z (MAR, MAY, JUL, DEC).

This chart pertains to the pricing of the DEC corn contract. This 15-year smoothed trend line is an approximation to illustrate the seasonal price tendencies of the DEC corn futures.

Seasonal CORN Prices of DEC Contract

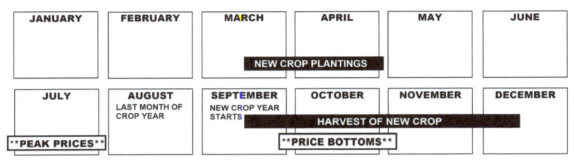

JANUARY	FEBRUARY	MARCH	APRIL	MAY	JUNE
		NEW CROP PLANTINGS			

JULY	AUGUST LAST MONTH OF CROP YEAR	SEPTEMBER NEW CROP YEAR STARTS	OCTOBER	NOVEMBER	DECEMBER
PEAK PRICES		HARVEST OF NEW CROP			
		PRICE BOTTOMS			

The world's two largest corn producing nations, the United States and China, lie in the Northern Hemisphere. These corn farmers are forced by the seasons into harvesting their corn in the final four months of the calendar year. This barrage of supply occurs over a period of about 12 weeks from mid-September into mid-December. Economics 101 - Supply/Demand: As the growing season of risk turns to harvest and an entire year's worth of global corn supply come to market - the DEC corn **contract prices bottom *during the last four months of the calendar year.*** Most often the bottom is in October. Conversely, corn is planted in the spring and the crop is at risk of drought, flood, and temperature/pollination during the summer months with a peak price for the DEC contract in May-July, most often in July. These price peaks are during the time that the new crop is still at risk, while the stocks of corn from the previous year are dwindling.

15 YEAR HISTORICAL AVERAGE SMOOTHED-LINE FOR DECEMBER CORN CONTRACT

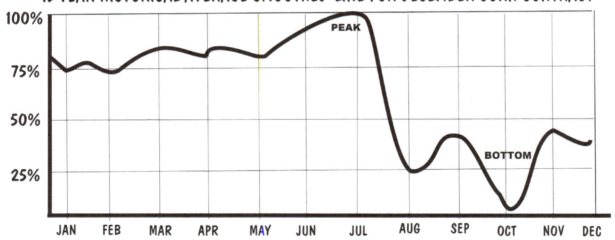

The left margin vertical axis is not the price but the percentage of the average prices over the 15-year price history of this contract.

Chapter 2 The Master Strategy in Selling Options

Our primary goal is to sell options. When you sell them (also called "writing options") the premium (the option's price) is credited to your trading account. If the options expire worthless, that money stays in your account. This would be "mission accomplished." In reality, there are often times when we sell an option, it's value goes down (a good thing), and we will exit the trade early (well before its expiration) by closing the trade. The reason is simple: If we sell an option for $700 and it's value has gone down to under $200, we might choose to buy it back for a $500 profit. Keeping the option, under these circumstances, would continue to risk our $500 profit in order to try to make the remaining $200. Some traders may feel confident enough to just let the trade expire and make the remaining $200; this is a trade decision call you will learn to make. If the option remains far OTM (out-of-the-money) and the option will almost certainly expire worthless (in your opinion), you can choose to try and keep the entire $700.

Nine Steps to Selected Commodity Option Selling

Think of these nine steps as your due diligence before placing a trade. We'll discuss each of these steps, and along the way, will further identify some other important characteristics of commodity options. You may modify some of these to suit your own style. For now, just consider these to be a working outline of the process.

1. Identify a price trend
2. Study the seasonal fundamentals of the underlying
3. Review news and (crop) reports
4. Identify unlikely price points within a given time-frame
5. Check IV% (options Implied Volatility) values
6. Choose a strike price and examine the price of the option(s)
7. Decide how many to sell and determine the margin requirements to be met
8. Form a trade-management plan, should the trade go against you

9. Make the trade

If your experience in trading options is primarily in stock options, you are going to notice a number of differences between that experience and learning to sell options on commodity futures contracts. Every thing you learned while trading stock options will not universally apply to options on futures.

Each of these parameters will be discussed, but first we'll address some more of the basics to get you ready to identify possible trades.

High Probability Trading

Fortunately, all the math will be done transparently by your trading platform. You only need to know how to understand and apply a few parameters.

The wonderful thing about this type of trading is that we do *not* have to portend where prices will go. We are going to be able to make money whether prices go up, down, or stay the same; this is the beauty of selling very far OTM (out-of-the-money) commodity options. If you've been trading options within short bursts of time, you are going to find this trading a slow change of pace. Rather than trying to outsmart a market, we are going to make money by just not doing stupid things – or as I like to call it "trading smarter."

Charlie Munger is Warren Buffett's partner and right-hand-man. He has said more than once that the success in making the billions of dollars that he and Warren have, is more "trying to be consistently not stupid, instead of trying to be very intelligent."

What we are going to do is to effectively use a three-tier criteria for selecting trades. You've seen the seasonal price tendencies for the DEC corn futures. Now we'll introduce the next step: Using the math that casinos and insurance companies use to make money. While you won't have to do any number crunching, it is important that you understand what is sometimes called the normal distribution of probability, most commonly illustrated by a Bell Curve with SD's (Standard Deviations) marked. There are entire books and courses on this subject and the ideas and applications around the concept resulted in a Nobel Prize. I'm only covering the basic concept here; it's all that's required for us, as we will choose to let our broker's software do the math for us.

The Black–Scholes model is a mathematical model of a financial market containing derivative investment instruments. From the model, one can deduce the Black–Scholes formula. The formula led to a boom in options trading and provided mathematical legitimacy to the activities of the Chicago Board Options Exchange and other options markets around the world (circa 1973).

If we know the number of days until expiration of an option and the volatility of the underlying, the Black-Scholes formula (or one of the refined equivalents) can be used to compute the theoretical value of an option. In other words, we can make some predictions about the value of an option over time. The option parameter on your trading software called "Prob OTM" (the probability an option will expire out-of-the-money) is a product of all this.

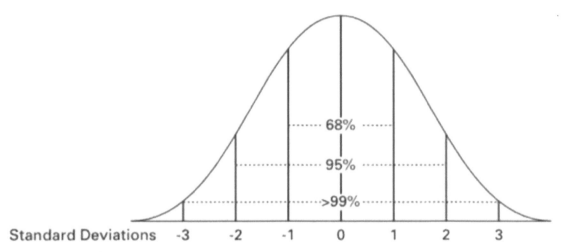

Standard Deviations   -3   -2   -1   0   1   2   3

Given a scenario input, there is a 68% probability a price will remain between +1 and -1 standard deviation. There's a 95% chance of a price remaining between +2 and -2 SD's, and a 99% change within +3 and -3 standard deviations.

So you see, we not only study the historical price behavior of a contract; additionally, we compute (your software does) the "Prob. OTM." I should point out that the total probability of a successful trade is a combination of the seasonal price behavior *and* this option modeling math, each being more or less independent of the other. We'll use both sets of information in our trading to sell far OTM options. Additionally, by having a trading plan, we will use prudent money management/ trade management guidelines. If all goes well, we'll have a perfectly boring trade that makes us a great return. If you are not a fan of math, no problem; as the old adage goes, you won't have to build a clock to know what time it is.

Why Commodity Options instead of Stock Options

A stock option controls the rights or obligations of 100 shares of stock.
A commodity option controls the right or obligations of 1 futures contract.

If we have a deposit of margin to trade a hundred shares of stock valued at $50 per share, the margin requirement is about 50% at $2500. The leverage is 2:1

To trade a contract of corn, the initial margin requirement (at the time of this writing) is about $825. DEC corn is about $4.05 per bushel, each contract represents 5,000 bushels, so the total value is $4.05 times 5,000 = $20,250. The leverage is (20255/825)= 24.5 to 1.

You can see that trading commodities has a leverage that is almost 12 times greater than stock trading. This high leverage allows a relatively small amount of money to control an underlying with a much greater value. Some futures contracts have margins that allow even higher leverage. In terms of how much money (margin money) we put up to trade, commodities have much more "bang per buck" than equities.

> The best opportunities in trading can be found, by using mathematically high odds when selecting trades, then coupling this with knowledge of periodically recurring natural seasonal price trends.

Summary:

1. Use Seasonal Trends to find Price Targets
2. Use Trading Platform to find "Prob. OTM" High Probability Trades
3. Take advantage of the high leverage of commodity futures and options

Please notice that none of the three items above have anything to do with the emotions of trading. Our Time-Farming goal is to sell options far OTM and to depend on the time decay of those options to slowly grow our profits.

Seasonal Implied Volatility

There is yet another parameter that can help improve the timing of a trade. It is the *seasonal trend in volatility*. You can see in the chart (Corn Price Volatility- 5-year History) that regular seasonal trends in volatility can be an integral part of the timing of a trade.

With options, one of the major components of the option's value is the IV% (implied volatility.) During times of faster changing prices, the IV% will increase. When the implied volatility of an option increases, the PRICE of the option also increases. This is why options sellers want to sell when IV% is HIGH, and buy when IV% is LOW. Often option traders can be correct about price direction and the IV% of an option will work against the trade.

When possible, option sellers should sell options when IV% is HIGH. Look at this chart of seasonal corn volatility. You see that IV% maximum occurs during JUN and JUL. Ideally, an option seller will sell when IV% is HIGH, and as the IV% seasonally decreases, the option seller will benefit.

Implied Volatility is directly proportional to option prices, so the ideal time to sell is when the IV% (implied vol.) is at it's peak.

When you sell CALL options, you want the underlying's price to go down, stay the same, or go up but never as high as the strike price of the CALLs.

When you sell options, you prefer the IV% to be at or near peak.

This chart illustrates how the seasonal volatility of corn peak in JUN/JUL each year.

Let's put this all together:

1. You use seasonal contract price trends.
2. Use mathematical "Prob OTM"
3. You take advantage of the high leverage of commodities.
4. Ideally, you sell options when the IV% is near a peak.

Every one of these, will get you closer to a winning trade. You must realize that it is rare to sell options when the IV% is at it's absolute peak, but the goal is to sell *near* the peak. The point here is not to sell options when IV% is low while it is trending higher; this works *against* your short option trades. Having said that, many times the Time Farming type trade can be so far OTM, we don't need to be overly concerned with changes in IV% (implied volatility.) Just remember while IV% is not always a primary factor in choosing these types of trades, it should not be ignored.

Time Decay

There is a force that can work *with* you as you trade. It is as predictable as gravity, as regular as the seasons, and as reliable as a count-down clock at New Year's Eve. It is called *time decay*.

Why do we sell options with expiration dates that are two to six month out? So we can collect time premium. Prices of the DEC corn contract usually peak in JUN, and then corn prices seasonally decline in the last four calendar months of the year (SEP, OCT, NOV, and DEC) for the DEC contract. The *time value* of the options we sell constantly declines. Think of it as a rental property that pays monthly. As time passes, the value of the options we sell continues to decrease. If we sell the option at peak implied volatility into declining volatility, and the time value also is decreasing, we are more likely to have profitable trades.

The time value *decay* of options that are months away from expiration increases exponentially as the date of expiration nears. The fastest time decay is in the last thirty days until expiration.

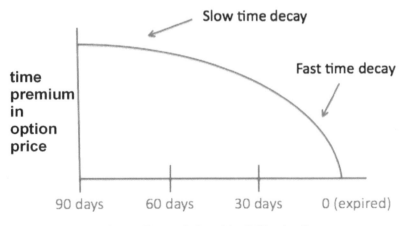

Time Remaining Until Expiration

13

We are using the DEC corn contract in the illustrations so far; please know that in the chapters that follow, other markets will be discussed. The first order of business in this book is to illustrate to you how to sell far OTM (Out-of-The-Money) commodity options. After you learn to identify the trade selection principles, that knowledge will easily transfer over to other commodities and futures products.

If you think that the more different kinds of trades you use and increasing the number of trades you make is the key to investing profits, then please think again. Selling far OTM commodity options and managing those trades is a very valuable skill; it likely requires an entirely different mindset for those who have been using price targets in trading. Where price-target trading is primarily a "shoot and hit or miss" method, Time Farming has a different goal altogether. Time Farming trading only has to approximate "where prices won't go" in order to produce a winning trade.

The commodity markets are less dependent on human beings than the stock markets. Basic commodities are natural resources and actual physical products and are less subject to manipulations. The prices of commodities are more likely to remain constant in any part of the world and the demand and supply is universal. Equities do not generally touch upon an individual's day to day life as do commodities. The masses are more concerned about the prices of crude oil and gasoline than they are about the price of a stock. The trends in a stock market are subjective and less sustainable as compared to commodity trends which are more predictable and long lasting.

Chapter 3 The Sweet Spot is Where Prices Won't Go

A regulation dart board is 18 inches in diameter. The center circle bulls-eye is a mere half-inch wide, less than one square inch. If you got paid $100 every time you pinned the bulls-eye but had to pay $10 for each dart you throw, most people would consider themselves lucky to break-even.

But what if you got paid $10 every time you hit any part of the board and had to pay $1 each time you missed the entire target? The "sweet spot" is now over 250 times larger! The odds are now overwhelmingly in your favor, even if you are a relatively inexperienced player. You get paid less for each success but you have a much larger target and higher probability of success. This is the winning principle of what I call *Time Farming*®.

Due to the high leverage of commodity trading, you can often sell CALL strikes that are up to 50% out-of-the-money for substantial premiums. Harmonizing your trades with seasonal price trends and coordinating trades with supply-demand fundamentals can identify price ranges in order to locate far OTM strikes with a high probability of expiring worthless. This is the essence of the Time Farming method.

Visit the illustration below: Let's suppose it is the first week of JUN, and the DEC corn contract is trading near 405 ($4.05/bushel) and since seasonal peak prices of this contract usually occur in MAY-JUL, we believe that, although prices could still go up more, the price is likely near the PEAK for the year (of the DEC corn contract.).

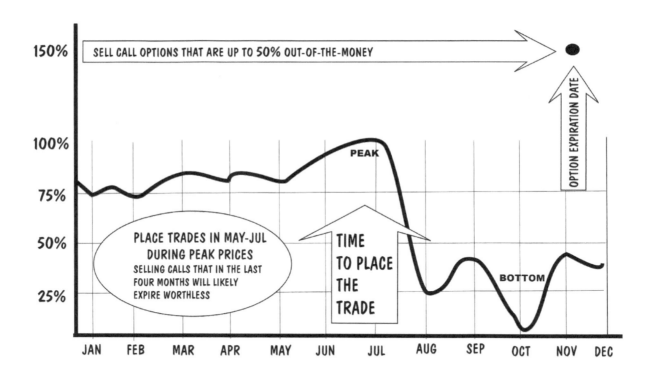

15 YEAR HISTORICAL AVERAGE SMOOTHED-LINE FOR DECEMBER CORN CONTRACT

Our goal is to find some CALL strikes on the DEC corn contract to SELL. The higher the strike, the less likely they would ever be in-the-money (or ever near the money.) We can look at a long-term chart (not shown here) and we find that at anytime during the last three years, the DEC corn contract has not traded higher than 473. 50% out-of-the-money strikes, with prices near 400 would be (400 x 1.5) = 600 strike. We check the present options price on the DEC corn contract and find a 600-strike, far OTM CALL that expires in 170 days sells for bid/ask: 1.375/1.625

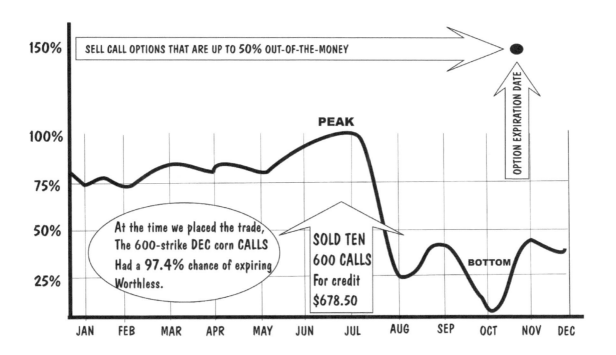

15 YEAR HISTORICAL AVERAGE SMOOTHED-LINE FOR DECEMBER CORN CONTRACT

One option is on one futures contract and each contract is 5,000 bushels of corn, so we can sell the option for 1.375 cents. Each penny of the price represents $50 (.01 times 5,000.) So 1.375 times $50 is equal to: $68.75 We choose to sell ten of the DEC Corn strike 600 CALLs for a total credit in our account of $687.50. Our trading software (doing the math for us) indicates the initial margin money to make this trade is: $952.50, so the trade could make a return of $687.50 on margin requirement of $952.50, about 687.5/952.5 (100)= 72.1% over the 171 days.

Trade Setup Strategies

This illustration used the strategy of "selling far OTM CALL options"; this is selling "naked" options since we do not own the underlying contract and there are no option combinations being traded to cover any of the risks. This risk of selling uncovered ("naked") options, is said to be "unlimited risk." There are other strategies that have less risk and less payout. There is no free lunch, gain is always commensurate with risk. Another strategy, which will be detailed ahead, is an option combination, the *vertical credit spread*. No matter which type of option trades you eventually use, the pursuit of suitable trade opportunities remains basically the same.

Margin Requirements

These types of trades can require *additional* margin money should the trade go against you or *less* margin money while the trade goes your way. The SPAN margin requirements in commodity trading are marked-to-the-market at each day's end of trading. These requirements (margins required for your trades) change each day. If you are new at commodity trading and do not fully understand how margin requirements are determined, you should talk with your broker's help line so you fully understand. You also need to know that the amount of margin requirement from one broker to another is not always the same. Individual brokerage companies can have individual policies and they have the right to control these amounts. In commodities trading, the amount of margin required can and does change from day-to-day. Wide swings in prices can result in substantial additional margin requirements; if you do not have the reserves in your account, you could get a call for an additional deposit. This is referred to as a "margin call."

note: Your trading software will show you the initial margin requirements BEFORE you place the trade. At this point you can just cancel the trade before it is "entered"; this is a quick and easy way to see the computed margin requirements of a trade before you make a final decision. This allows you to reset if you wish to change the number of options you will consider setting, change to another strike, or to change any of the trade parameters.

Almost all the on-line brokers have a free "paper-trading" account customers can use to practice trades and test ideas without risking real money. If you are trading in one of the discounted on-line brokers, you do not have the advantage of having a live person on the phone "holding your hand" and discussing trades with you while you learn. If you are going to use a discount broker, be sure you use the practice account and your brokers help line to learn how to create and manage trades before you use real money. This type of trading isn't for everyone and it can be especially risky unless you gain experience with many of the methods described in this book. Many traders are quite happy paying more in commissions in order to have a live broker assist them. Also there are specialized brokers who routinely handle these types of trades and they accept qualified clients and will handle all the details for you. Unless you have experience trading futures and options, be sure you do your homework so you won't be in for any unpleasant surprises.

This trading is highly leveraged, and works very differently than just trading stocks. One of the most common mistakes of commodity traders, especially rookies, is over leveraging, trading out of one's comfort zone. Even though you may execute high probability trades, sooner or later some of those will go against you. The old adage "expect the best but prepare for the worst" is apropos. If you are new to commodity and commodity option trading, I recommend "baby steps" until you gain experience and confidence.

If you do have experience in trading commodities and commodity options and but are new to these "Time Farming" methods (selling options and using option combinations instead of the outright buying of options), then I suspect you are in for a unique experience. While "trading smarter" may require a little more work and research, these efforts can payoff by trading with much less risk than trying to guess price, market direction, and the timing required for successful option buying.

Order your free bonus chapter for this book now. Just send me an email to Don@WriteThisDown.com and put TIME FARMING in the subject line to receive the free PDF file. This includes important resource links for research, tips on selecting trades, and suggestions for money management when time farming.

Chapter 4 Vertical Credit Spreads

Vertical Credit Spreads are an easy strategy to learn:

- You get an immediate credit in your account and that amount is your maximum profit.
- Risk is limited. You know your max loss and max margin requirement at the time you enter the trade.
- Your Probability of Profit is easy to calculate.

Vertical Call Credit Spread – using CALLs and you have a *bearish* opinion of the market direction

Vertical Put Credit Spread – using PUTs and you have a *bullish* opinion of the market direction

Vertical CALL Credit Spreads for Bearish Markets

To keep things simple, we'll continue with the middle-of-the-year seasonal Corn scenario: We place a trade during JUN or JUL while seasonal prices are near a peak, near $4.00 per bushel in this illustration. (Of course this varies from season to season, even though the regular DEC Corn contract typically does peak at this time of year, unless the trends are counter-seasonal.) And please remember, we are using data on only one of the corn contracts, the DEC Corn contract price history over the last 15 years.

We expect the DEC corn contract in our illustration to follow normal seasonal trends, peaking in JUN/JUL and then declining as harvest progresses during the last four calendar months of the year. This next illustration assumes we are placing a trade in mid-year, in JUN, and we are selling options on the (still six months out) DEC futures contract.

From our broker's trading platform (not shown here), we look at the DEC Corn contracts, DEC options. With DEC corn trading at 400 cents/bushel, we see a far OTM 500 CALL is trading at 5.5 cents ($50 x 5.5 = $272.50) and we look at another strike, the 540-strike even farther OTM is trading for 2.5 cents ($50 x 2.5 = $112.50). We SELL the 500-strike while simultaneously BUYING the 540-strike, and the net CREDIT placed in our account of $272.50 minus $112.50 = Credit of: $150.

VERTICAL CALL CREDIT SPREAD

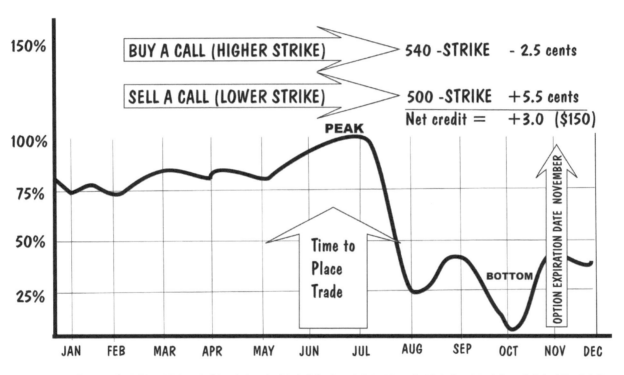

15 YEAR HISTORICAL AVERAGE SMOOTHED-LINE FOR DECEMBER CORN CONTRACT

This figure illustrates our Vertical CALL Credit Spread with the option combination short the 500-CALL and long the 540 CALL for a net credit of $150 collected. The initial margin requirement is about $90 per spread. Time until expiration is about 170 days.

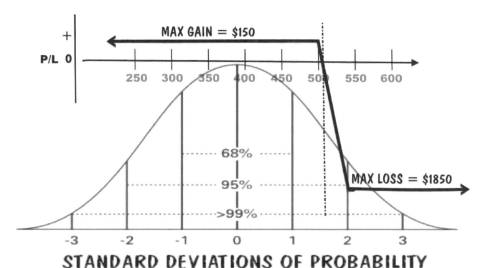

VERTICAL CALL CREDIT SPREAD
BEARISH MARKET VIEW

SELL 1 DEC Corn 500 strike CALL for credit of 5.50 (+$272.50)
BUY 1 DEC Corn 540 strike CALL for debit of 2.50 (- $112.50)
A NET Credit of (5.50 minus 2.50) = 3.0 = $150
Maximum Loss: [(540-500) - 3.00] = 37= $1850
89% Prob. of 500 Call expiring OTM
Break-Even = 500 + 3 = 503

MAX GAIN = $150

P/L 0

250   300   350   400   450   500   550   600

68%

95%

>99%

MAX LOSS = $1850

-3   -2   -1   0   1   2   3

STANDARD DEVIATIONS OF PROBABILITY

In this illustration, you see the maximum loss is $1850. Since the loss is limited (though not probable), the $1850 is the maximum margin you could be required to post, even though the

23

initial margin to place the trade is about $90 per spread. The **STANDARD DEVIATIONS OF PROBABILITY** superimposed over the P/L (profit/loss) of the trade is an approximation to show the probability of price moves in the DEC corn futures price. This is just a visual way to say that these far OTM options are likely to expire worthless. The actual probability of the 500-strike CALL expiring OTM is about 90% (This number is computed automatically by your trading platform). As you examine the options and prices when you are placing the trade, each strike option has a parameter (usually designated as) "Prob.OTM."

Trade Management

This is a good place to discuss some trade management techniques and guidelines. The initial margin is about $90 per spread. Margin requirements (the cash you must have in your account to cover the risk) are determined by recalculations (automatically) at the close of trading each day. Since, at the time of placing the trade, DEC corn is trading at about 400, the 500-strike option very far OTM. Due to this, if the DEC corn contract varies by 5 or 10 cents in a day, the margin requirements won't change much at all. On the other hand, if the DEC corn prices go up higher over a period of time, your margin requirement can increase all the way up to the max risk amount of $1850. If during the trade – the price of the spread you sold should increase to double the credit you received, which would be about $300, you may wish to consider taking the loss of about $150 and closing the trade. (Remember you already received $150 when you placed the trade, so your loss if the spread value doubles is $300 minus $150.)

While we would all want our trade management to be perfectly clear and exact, it does require some thought as your trade is in progress. If this seasonal trade is going against you, you may use the above example as a *guideline* to exit. If the fundamentals of a commodity have, or are undergoing significant changes that will drastically increase the risk of the trade, the 2:1 is a good rule-of-thumb. As you gain experience, you'll get better at these types of judgement calls, but being either hopeful or over-confident can be destructive to your account balance. Each person's risk tolerance and ability to balance multiple sources of data is unique. Even as you become a more seasoned and experienced trader you will not always make the correct and profitable decision. After the trade is done, you will be able to look back with 20-20 hindsight and see what you should have done. Don't beat yourself up this way because you can never have the same information *during* a trade that you have *after* the trade has long been over. You try to detach emotionally, and make decisions with the information you have at hand. The tendency we all have to "let trades run" when they aren't going our way can be very costly. What is needed is to learn to exit the trade with losses you can easily absorb, take the hit and move on to a more profitable scenario. No one will win them all, ever! After all, the experience of "exiting a trade" is really having to admit all the preparation and thought we made could not overcome factors that we have no control over. This is a theme of life in general, not just in trading. Be nice to yourself and preserve your capital for future trades. Never "revenge trade", or doubling up and then hoping for things to get better, these emotions are a recipe for disaster.

While it is unlikely the DEC corn futures price will go into a counter-seasonal price pattern, it can and does happen on rare occasion. Suppose for instance, the mid America corn belt experiences deep flooding, this could potentially destroy a portion of the crop or make it impossible to harvest in a timely manner.

There are many free resources on the internet to get the USDA crop reports and there are a number of websites that post daily commentaries on crop conditions, weather, planting and harvest progressions. Those planting and harvest progressions will compare the current season's progress with an average "normal" (in percentages) season. Just the threat of flooding (or other negative factors) can cause the futures prices to fluctuate. International trade treaties can be subject to changes that can effect prices, as can disruptions in crop growth, harvest, and distribution. When you consider these factors, you can understand how you must follow your trades closely. A later chapter in this book will show you some ways to collect and use other crop and seasonal parameters like ending stocks, crop yield projections, foreign market production, acreage planted compared to other seasons, and amounts of carryover stocks from the old seasons harvest (amounts in storage.)

If you are new to this type of trading, this may seem like a lot of learning and work, and it can be. Remember, while you are placing trades with a high probability of success, there is no "free lunch". You must do your homework and it requires both time and effort. If it didn't everybody would be doing it. Farmers are normally hard-working people, and becoming a "Time Farmer" also requires knowledge and work. This type of trading can be very profitable but those profits must often be earned. After a year or two, it may seem like a lot less work because you become more fluent at managing these trades. This type of trading, for all these reasons, is not for everybody.

Option Combination Trades

Just to give you a working frame of reference here, you should know that the Vertical Credit Spread is an *option combination* trade, the simultaneous trading of two or more different options at once. There are literally 50 or more kinds of option combination trades; fortunately, you won't need to learn but two or three to accomplish the trading described in this book. Veteran option traders usually stick to a few strategies that become their favorites, even though they might be proficient at using any of them. Learning a new strategy for option combinations is usually done one at a time, as you need them or choose to learn additional types of trading. *If you are new to option trading, trying to learn them all at once is very confusing and often futile* (counter productive.)

If you are new to using this strategy, the *vertical credit spread*, you should know that your broker's trading platform makes it easy to place these trades. The trading software has a special provisions to select and trade each of the types of option combinations. Your broker has free instructional videos to help you learn to use these features in your trading platform. If you are fuzzy about what you need, call the help line and tell them you plan to place some vertical credit spreads, and have them direct you to the proper instructional video. No need to be shy, trading platforms are powerful and have hundreds of features. Almost everyone needs assistance from time-to-time. Don't expect the help line to validate your choice of trades, or to recommend trade specifics; they can't legally do that – and it just isn't their job. They can talk in hypothetical terms and use illustrations in helping you learn, but your broker's help line is not intended to be any sort of trade advisory service. Most of these great people are very patient, professional, and knowledgeable people; they do a terrific job and they have many resources to help you learn that have been put together at great cost.

The types of option combinations discussed in the book are limited to:

Vertical Credit Spreads: Bear spreads using CALLs and Bull spreads using PUTs.
Ratio Credit Spreads, also in Bear and Bull scenarios.

Vertical PUT Credit Spreads for Bullish Markets

The next illustration will show you how to place a vertical PUT Credit spread for a seasonal play in the Unleaded Gasoline (RBOB) JUL contract. The average seasonal price trend for unleaded gasoline prices is historically strong, but this is a good time to remind you that counter-seasonal years do happen, and you should do all your research to try to confirm that you are correctly placing your trade in accordance with the current year's trends. The largest influence on these JUL Unleaded Gasoline prices (symbol is RB) is the price of crude oil. Associative alliances with world oil producers (such as OPEC) can easily affect prices, and you must be aware of these factors, the timing of announcements and negotiations, if any. Over the last 25 years, threats to supplies, transportations disruptions, economic sanctions, civil wars, international interventions, and other factors have at time been a major influence in crude oil and thus gasoline prices. Since this trade will be selling PUT options into a bullish price scenario, it does help to know that most of the surprises and disruptions would likely cause prices to go UP, not down (which would be "good" for our vertical PUT credit spread.)   Whether in agricultural or energy markets, you never want to fly blindly into seasonal trades without carefully studying the present news and context of prices in a market.

In an energy market like crude oil or gasoline, it is possible you might be considering this seasonal trade at a time when prices have already abnormally increased in a counter-seasonal move; this can make a trade unexpectedly unattractive. In a case like this, prices could decrease in a counter-seasonal move. When considering seasonal trades, you must do all research to try to confirm that normal seasonal patterns apply during the timing of your trades, OR that you can seek a trade that works in a counter-seasonal price pattern.

Ideas for Research Resources

No matter which market(s) you are trading, keep in mind that with the Time Farming method, selling far OTM options, we don't have to be completely right about price movements, we just have to be "not wrong." This takes some of the pressure off, but experienced traders never take things for granted, they always do due diligence and research prior to placing the trade, and to understand how to manage a trade while its in progress.

A rookie-mistake is to get overloaded with too much information, much of it extraneous; this is called "analysis paralysis." If you are new to this type of trading, always keep it simple. There are times when no matter how much you want to place a (seasonal) trade, the pieces just aren't fitting together. When you experience this, remember that there are always other markets and trades. To paraphrase Warren Buffett, *the markets are a way of transferring money from the impatient to the patient.*

Government reports are a prime source of information on commodity markets. For energy, The US Energy and Information Administration is a prime resource. It is free of course, and the information and reports issued there strongly influence prices. Log on to the site and explore all the resources. You will often through other channels find analysis based on the information here. **http://www.eia.gov/petroleum/supply/weekly/**

Of course, unless you already know and trust a source of market analysis, you should read/listen to several sources until you find resources you feel you can trust. I would caution you against merely reacting to a few headlines you hear on any of the financial channels or newspaper/magazines. Remember you are running your own business and you should be relentless in seeking multiple and reliable sources before putting your money at risk.

A Seasonal Unleaded Gasoline Vertical PUT Bullish Credit Spread

SEASONAL RBOB GASOLINE JUL CONTRACT

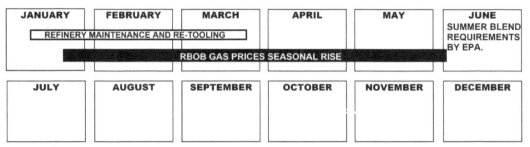

Gas prices generally peak around Memorial Day. Several factors contribute to this annual increase including, refinery maintenance, the switch to summer-blend fuels which are more expensive to produce and an increase in demand as more people begin traveling in the spring and summertime. Crude oil prices are the biggest factor driving gas prices, but how the crude oil is processed also plays a significant role in price increases. The petroleum industry's switchover to summer-blend fuels, a process that begins each February and ends June 1, creates challenges that also affect retail fuels prices. Since final implementation of the Clean Air Act Amendments in 2000, the seasonal transition to summer-blend fuel has helped gasoline prices climb significantly before they reached their peak. SOURCE:THE ASSOCIATION FOR CONVENIENCE & FUEL RETAILING www.nacsonline.com

15-YEAR HISTORICAL AVERAGE SMOOTHED-LINE FOR THE JULY CONTRACT OF RBOB GASOLINE

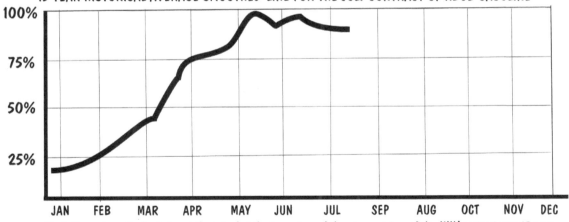

The left margin vertical axis is not the price but the percentage of the average prices of the JULY contract over 15 years.

29

RBOB Gasoline Futures Contract Specifications

Contract Unit	42,000 gallons	
Price Quotation	U.S. dollars and cents per gallon	
Trading Hours	CME Globex:	Sunday - Friday 6:00 p.m. - 5:00 p.m. (5:00 p.m. - 4:00 p.m. Chicago Time/CT) with a 60-minute break each day beginning at 5:00 p.m. (4:00 p.m. CT)
	CME ClearPort:	Sunday - Friday 6:00 p.m. - 5:00 p.m. (5:00 p.m. - 4:00 p.m. Chicago Time/CT) with a 60-minute break each day beginning at 5:00 p.m. (4:00 p.m. CT)
Minimum Price Fluctuation	$0.0001 per gallon	
Product Code	CME Globex: RB CME ClearPort: RB Clearing: RB TAS: RBT	
Listed Contracts	Monthly contracts listed for the current year and the next 3 calendar years +1 month. Monthly contracts for a new calendar year will be added following the termination of trading in the December contract of the current year.	
Settlement Method	Deliverable	
Termination Of Trading	Trading in a current delivery month shall cease on the last business day of the month preceding the delivery month.	

Trade Setup: In the first quarter of the calendar year and up to Memorial Day at the end of May, the JULY contract of RBOB gasoline prices have a seasonal pattern of price increases. We would look to place this trade during seasonal lows, usually in mid-January to the middle of February. There are years when this low can occur at a different interval (as early as NOV for example.) When you are anticipating this seasonal trade (or any seasonal trade in other markets), you should pay attention to trends year round, study and follow the markets. If prices are not indicating seasonal lows near this time, you may want to pass on this strategy, or at least be more careful in selecting your strikes to sell. Our goal is to try and pinpoint where JUL RBOB gasoline prices WON'T go. You may find you are selling PUT strikes when prices are going lower or are already low – at a time that is heading into seasonal peaks in the months ahead.

RBOB. Acronym. Definition.
RBOB. Reformulated Blendstock for Oxygenate Blending (gasoline production) The most commonly traded blends of gasoline.

RBOB GASOLIINE FUTURES
contract = 42,000 gal
Min. Price fluctuation = $.0001 = $4.20

JUL 2017	1.6310	+0.0291

A change of +0.0291 equals 291 X $4.20 = $1,222.20 or $420 per penny per gallon

Peak seasonal demand for gasoline in North America and Europe is in the late spring and summer months when the weather is good for automobile travel and for popular outdoor activities. Peak prices during peak demand, economics 101.

The buildup occurs in the months just prior to peak demand as refineries are re-tooling for summer blends and building stocks to sell product in the months ahead.

We are going to sell a PUT far OTM (way below current prices), and then simultaneously buy another PUT ever farther OTM to limit our risk to a finite amount.

Here's an example (see chart: **JULY 2015 RBOB Gasoline**): In July 2014, the high for this JUL15 contract was made. Six months later, January 12th, the seasonal LOW was made. Of course with this chart, since we are looking back in time, we have the advantage of 20-20 hindsight. In reality, we would have probably waited for some indication of a seasonal upturn in prices and/or we would be convinced by normal seasonal fundamental information that at least the price on or around mid-January was near a seasonal LOW. The MACD histogram might help you locate a near bottom area (note this chart is plotting weekly over a three year period).

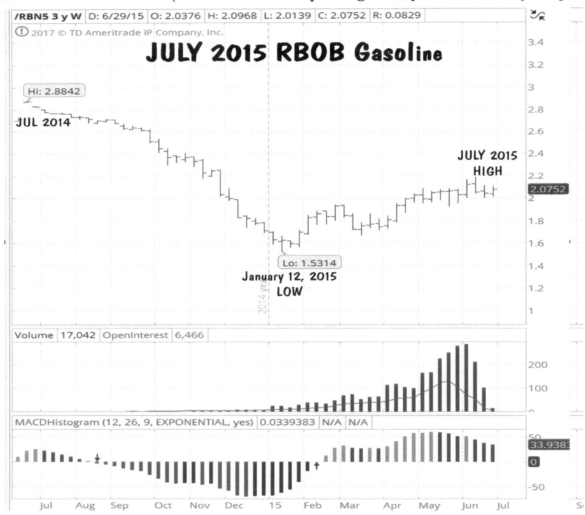

Please remember, one of the beautiful things about working these seasonal trades is that we do not need to be able to pick an exact bottom; *we are only required to be right about where prices won't go.* This gives us a luxury we seldom have in any price-targeting types of trades; the timing of our trade often becomes much easier. For example: In setting up this seasonal trade for the JUL2015 RBOB gasoline: We might not have placed the trade near the bottom on January 12, 2015. Even as late as the month of March would have worked well. We might have sold the JUL15 1.5-strike PUT and bought the (farther OTM) 1.4-strike PUT to complete our Vertical Bull Credit Spread using PUT options.

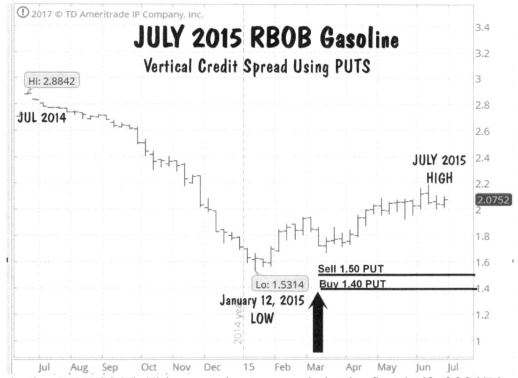

Note this is the JULY **2015.** This next chart example in the first half of **2017** is counter-seasonal:

RBOB JULY-2017 Counter-Seasonal Trend

RBOB JUL2017 CONTRACT
Unleaded Gasoline JAN through JUNE OF 2017
COUNTER-SEASONAL TREND

Although 15-year averages indicated JULY RBOB prices normally increase from JAN to JUL, this chart of the JUL-2017 RBOB contract price was clearly counter-seasonal (JAN to JUL in 2017.) This counter-seasonal price swing was attributed to large inventories of oil, and the ability of US producers using evolving technology to lower the cost of domestic oil production. During this time period, the price of Crude Oil dropped from about $58 to $43 dollars a barrel. Fracking technology produces domestic crude at about $25 a barrel; just a few years ago, that break-even was $45 to $50 per barrel. Again, technology brings huge changes to a market that brings in a new paradigm of pricing.

This illustrates very well why you should never fly blindly into trading of any markets by using only historical price trends. It is a beginner's mistake to trade historical price trends without researching the fundamentals of a market. Commodity markets, unlike stocks, are a physical product. Production, inventories, demand, and a myriad of other reasons drive prices overwhelmingly more than any technical indicators, particularly over a period of time.

Confirming a Seasonal Trend Before You Place a Trade

If you are an experienced trader, you know how easy charts can make trading look, so long as you are back-testing ideas. In fact, many people who advertise these miraculous-sounding claims that tout "easy road to riches" trading "secrets" are simply giving you results of past events. Please beware of these smooth pitches that try to lure you into believing you can buy the "Holy Grail of Trading." Even though they tell you that "you have nothing to lose", they might refund the fee you paid them, but they do not cover your losses!

In the example chart (on a previous page: **JULY 2015 RBOB Gasoline**), the chart shows a near perfect seasonal trade setup. That's what it is *supposed* to look like. In real-time trading, we never know "how low is low" and "how high is high" at any given moment. So how do you know if prices are, as you hope, in a somewhat "normal seasonal pattern?" One of the things you do first is look at a 15 year history of the specific contract you plan to trade (in our example, this is RBN5, the July 2015 RBOB.) In reality, this is a great start but you will have to do more. Since you are going to put real money on a trade, the cost of downloading and printing out, all individual price history charts of the JUL RB contract is just pennies. Get all 15 charts (give or take) and study them. Almost certainly, you will see the majority do indeed follow the normal seasonal pattern, but you might learn just as much from studying the charts where prices deviate from this norm. Having seen some seasonal variations by looking at all these will very likely help you make a more informed trading decision.

Most traders won't simply decide to do one of these seasonal trades just a day before he wants to place a trade; in fact, good traders are always looking ahead, following the contract progress of the ones she/he will be trading. This forward-looking trader will also be following the market fundamentals closely. Stepping into a commodity trade and only using technical charting to do it, can be very, very risky. Technical purist will insist that "all the fundamentals are built-in" to market pricing. If you like jumping off a cliff blindfolded, it's a great way to trade commodities. If you want to trade smart commodities, you will use fundamentals, technicals, government reports, commentary that you trust, and you will gain valuable experience as you go.

Plus experienced traders have another huge advantage: They often know when NOT to trade. Have you ever hear the expression, "All dressed up and there's no place to go."? When you study a contract for months, learn its history, read the fundamentals almost every day for weeks, follow it on charts, check the option prices, and get totally prepared --- When you have done all this and the data unexpectedly doesn't look good, you DO NOT trade. I am sorry to be the one that has to tell you, but sometimes this happens. When it does, just be glad you made the right decision. There's no reason to "force" a trade just because you are invested in prep time. Sometimes there are just factors over which you have no control; don't let emotions rule your game. Simply move on to fertile ground. Be glad you were smart to make the correct call. Trading can be fickle, sometimes you pass on a trade and you'll be wrong. Handle it the same way, move on and find fertile ground to plant your money in the next trade. The trades you "woulda, shoulda, coulda" made are water under the bridge.

While we are on the subject, you recall that a good rule of thumb to manage these trades in Time Farming is to cut your losses at twice the net amount you received when you sold your option (or combination). The number-one danger to any trading account is letting losses run and substituting hope (aka: good money after bad) for things to turn around. As Mark Twain said, "Denial isn't just a river in Egypt;" it can be very expensive. "Hope" is not a strategy.

The trades we are placing in Time Farming are far OTM trades. This has an inherent advantage; if things begin to go against us, we usually have plenty of time to get out of the way. Remember time is our friend; we live for time to pass and options to lose their value through time decay and slow, regular, seasonal price patterns. Normally, the trades we are placing are far enough OTM that they can't turn on us quickly, as so many other kinds of trading can do. If you are going to get caught standing on the railroad track and you see a train coming, you want to be so far away that you can easily take your time and just get out of the way. If you are selling strikes too close to the money, your "escape reaction time" gets limited quickly. Settle for making a little less money on the trade and putting the odds more deeply in your favor. Our goal in time-farming is to stay away from high risk, not to brush up against it and risk larger losses.

Another resource you can use to try to confirm seasonal price movements is to find a few experts who offer commentary on the markets you are trading. Several of the major universities in the grain belt have some free services with commentary on many farm commodities. There are brokers who specialize in markets that offer commentary on them; they wish to gain new customers by posting reliable data for traders. If you are new to trading commodities, I would suggest you take time to explore many of these choices before you spend money. There are also commercial services that offer reliable charts and data on seasonal spreads and contracts; many of these will offer a free trial period, so you can make sure what they provide is what you need. While they may not offer specific trade recommendations, they may have everything you need to make your own decisions.

There are some links in the free bonus material I can send you. To receive it simple send me an email with TIME FARMING in the subject line to: Don@WriteThisDown.com

Our subscription newsletter, *Monthly Training Bulletin*, also post useful links and articles. See: **TimeFarming.com**

The VERTICAL BULL CREDIT SPREAD and VERTICAL BEAR CREDIT SPREAD are PASSIVE DIRECTIONAL TRADES. All you have to do to make money is not be wrong.

Chapter 5 Using USDA Reports Fundamentals

Here is a 15-year price history of the NOV contract of Soybeans. Prices normally start rising in February and reach a seasonal Peak around JUN/JULY before dropping off the second half of the calendar year:

SEASONAL SOYBEAN PRICES NOV CONTRACT

The soybean market is dominated by two major producers: Brazil and the United States. Soybeans are harvested in November-December in the U.S., while the Brazil harvest takes place in May-June. Most of the U.S. crop is sold soon after harvest, driving prices down. Some of the crop is held until spring, hoping for better prices. US farmers need to raise cash for the spring planting and to make storage room for new crop. So in mid/late winter the remainder of stock are sold and the annual low prices occur, often in February. The Brazilian harvest will not reach the markets until June-July.

15-YEAR SEASONAL PRICE OF NOV CONTRACT SOYBEANS SMOOTHED-LINE APPROXIMATION

The left margin vertical axis is not the price but the percentage of the average prices of the JULY contract over 15 years.

Soybean Contract Specifications

Contract Unit	5,000 bushels (~136 metric tons)
Price Quotation	Cents per bushel
Trading Hours	Sunday – Friday, 7:00 p.m. – 7:45 a.m. CT and Monday – Friday, 8:30 a.m. – 1:20 p.m. CT
Minimum Price Fluctuation	1/4 of one cent per bushel ($12.50 per contract)
Product Code	CME Globex: ZS CME ClearPort: S Clearing: S TAS: SBT
Listed Contracts	January (F), March (H), May (K), July (N), August (Q), September (U) & November (X)
Settlement Method	Deliverable
Termination Of Trading	The business day prior to the 15th calendar day of the contract month.

Here's a chart (**SOYBEANS NOVEMBER CONTRACT 2017**) of the years 2014, 2015, and 2016, all of which have relatively normal seasonal price trends peaking in JUL. As you can see 2017 peaked early in the year (JAN to MAR) and began a very notable counter-seasonal downtrend in 2017. *Specifically, NOV contract prices are dropping off the first-half of the year - instead of during the usual second half of the year JUL to NOV time period.* Time-Farming is a long-term method of trading and we really don't care where prices are going, all we have to do is figure out where *they are not likely to go*. There is a perfectly real and logical reason this counter-seasonal trend is taking place in 2017. To understand it, we'll look at the *fundamentals* of this market for the 2017 counter-seasonal price trend.

Fundamental Crop Analysis

We are choosing to sell options several months out in time; this makes us *long term commodity traders*. Long-term trading in commodity markets is very heavily based on *fundamental analysis of supply and demand*. A market's fundamentals give us the big picture and some sense of perspective as to why prices are behaving as they are. Technically, soybeans are an oilseed but they are generally grouped with the "grains" as commodity markets are discussed, the other primary grains being corn, oats, and wheat. In this group each commodity contract is 5,000 bushels, the price quotes are in cents/bushel, and they all share the same trading hours. All of the grains are planted annually, unlike crops like orange juice that have trees that can produce for decades. When grain prices are high, farmers plant more (acres) of them to make more money. Then, as supply-demand becomes more balanced, prices begin to reflect that by moderating.

The USDA (United States Department of Agriculture) has domestic offices and attachés all over the world that report information. They will even put you on a free email list to receive the reports that you request, see:
https://apps.fas.usda.gov/psdonline/app/index.html#/app/home

The information in these reports is very important to track domestic and international supply and demand. Periodic scheduled reports, usually monthly, can and do influence commodity pricing. Here's another link for free USDA reports out of Cornell University:

http://usda.mannlib.cornell.edu/MannUsda/viewDocumentInfo.do?documentID=1194

The importance and value of these USDA reports for those trading commodities cannot be overemphasized. Get familiar with the monthly reports, especially the dates they are issued, for these reports often have a great impact on prices. While individual commodity markets can be quite different, the way the USDA reports crop conditions, stocks, import/export progress and expectations, crop yields, and acreage planted is very consistent. This means as you learn to follow the USDA reporting for one market, you can apply most of what you learn to other markets (in terms of the formatting in reading and evaluating the USDA reports.) All of the data centers around the basics of supply-demand; these reports supply valuable information that help one understand price behavior. For the Time Farming method of selling far OTM options, we need not portend exact price behavior (price-targets or the exact timing of them), nor must we try to find exact lows/highs, or reversals.

If you do not have experience using USDA reports and reading various private commentary of analyst and brokers, you should invest some of your time into studying them (start with the markets you are considering trading). Of the private commentary on crops, and there are hundreds of people and companies that issue them, some are very reliable and, as you might expect, some of them are not. Commonly, some of these commentators will specialize in following categories such as grains, energy, precious metals, softs, or other areas. Please understand that *commentary* and *trade advisories* can be mutually exclusive or they might be combined. The purest form of commentary is just fundamental information interpretation

– and the reader, whether a commercial producer or individual trader, is left to draw their own conclusions about what, if any, trading positions might produce individual results.

The commodity market for soybeans is an international one. The primary producers are the U.S. and Brazil. Due to geography, the timing for planting and harvesting is a virtual mirror image in the respective Northern and Southern Hemispheres. If you are new to commodity trading, you must learn the composition of individual markets. Rarely, is one person an expert in all of these markets, nor does one person expect to trade them all. Generally speaking, if you can find three to six markets and learn their fundamentals well enough to trade them, you have the potential to do very well. Frankly, it can take a lot of time and experience to successfully trade even a few markets. There are money management services that provide trading for high-net-worth individuals who can do the trading and research for you. There are also full-service brokers that can work with individual clients to assist with trading ideas and evaluations. There are research and data firms from which you can purchase charts, data, and sometimes commentary and there are a lot of free information resources available.

Since anyone who wants to can post commentaries, you are left on your own to evaluate how much of this – and which parts – may or may not be useful and/or accurate for your trading.

Now we are going to examine the fundamentals in the 2017 season of soybeans, a counter-seasonal price move, and a look at the fundamentals that drive this market. After studying these fundamentals, our example will show how options can be sold during this counter-seasonal year example. Remember, this commentary is from May 2017, and (at that time) a counter-seasonal pattern for the NOV 2017 contract.

SOYBEAN CONVERSION FACTORS

1 metric ton of soybeans = 36.74 bushels
1 bushel = .0272155 metric ton
1 Million Metric ton = 36.74 million bushels

SOYBEANS: The May 2017 USDA Supply/demand report for soybeans was considered mixed with the 2016-17 U.S. ending stocks at 435 million bushels compared to the estimate of 443 million (417-513 range). The 2017-18 U.S. ending stocks came in at just 480 million bushels compared to the average estimate of 584 million bushels (420-759 range). The USDA has increased exports for the new crop season to 2.150 billion bushels, up 100 million from this year even with the record South American crops. Crush is also higher. The 2016-17 World ending stocks came in at a record high 90.14 million tonnes versus the estimate of 87 million tonnes (86-89 range). The 2017-18 World ending stocks came in at 88.8 million tonnes versus the average estimate of 87 million tonnes (81-94 range). 2016-17 Brazilian soybean production came in at 111.6 million tonnes compared to the average estimate of 111.3 million tonnes (110.5-113.0 range). 2016-17 Argentine production came in at 57 million tonnes versus the average estimate of 56.0 million tonnes (55.0-57.0 range).

PRICE OUTLOOK: With record world ending stocks for the 2016/17 season due to surging South America production, the USDA still pushed crush and exports higher for the new crop season and the export number is a big surprise. With old crop world ending stocks up 3 million tonnes from expectations, it is difficult to call the news supportive. Consider selling November soybeans against trend line resistance at 980 with an objective of 930.

USDA SUPPLY/DEMAND US SOYBEANS	May USDA 15-16	Apr USDA 16-17	May USDA 16-17	May USDA 17-18
Area (M Acres)				
Planted	82.7	83.4	83.4	89.5
Harvested	81.7	82.7	82.7	88.6
Yield (Bu/Acre)	48.0	52.1	52.1	48.0
Beginning Stocks (M Bu)	191	197	197	435
Production	3,926	4,307	4,307	4,255
Imports	24	25	25	25
Supply, Total	4,140	4,528	4,528	4,715
Crushings	1,886	1,940	1,925	1,950
Exports	1,936	2,025	2,050	2,150
Seed	97	104	104	101
Residual	25	14	14	34
Use, Total	3,944	4,083	4,093	4,235
Ending Stocks	197	445	435	480
Stocks/Use Ratio	5.0%	10.9%	10.6%	11.3%

USDA SUPPLY/DEMAND WORLD SOYBEANS (Million Metric Tons)	May USDA 15-16	Apr USDA 16-17	May USDA 16-17	May USDA 17-18
Supply				
Beginning Stocks	77.37	77.13	77.08	90.14
Production	313.05	345.97	348.04	344.68
Imports	133.40	140.05	140.90	147.76
Use				
Crush, Domestic	275.56	291.95	290.68	301.53
Total Domestic	314.53	332.42	331.29	344.21
Exports	132.22	143.30	144.60	149.56
Ending Stocks	77.08	87.41	90.14	88.81
Stocks/Use Ratio	24.5%	26.3%	27.2%	25.8%

**SOYBEANS
NOVEMBER CONTRACT 2017**

2014 HIGH

Hi: 1130

2015 HIGH

2016 HIGH

2017 HIGH

COUNTER-SEASONAL

Lo: 857

This is the THREE-YEAR chart of NOV2017 Soybeans on June 1, 2017 ZSX7 is trading at 916

The options matrix for the NOV2017 Soybean options (next page) indicates that the 1400-strike CALL option has a 96.97% probability of expiring OTM. "Last X" (last traded) at 3.875 or (3.875 x $50) = $193.75 each and the bid/ask is 3.875 / 4.000, which is $193.75 / $200.00

As you can see rather easily on this option matrix, the 1400 CALLs are 50% Out-Of-the-Money. Selling 10 of these naked 1400-strike CALLs would be a credit in your account of $1937.50.   The initial margin on this trade would be about $2777 and the time until expiration is 141 days, about five calendar months.   The yield on the trade is $1937.50/$2777 = 69.7%. This is an annualized return of about 151%. In the option matrix, the strikes of 1300, 1360, and 1400 are marked. Use this matrix and compute what profits and probabilities these strikes offer the investor. Note the 1300-strike is still far OTM and has a Prob.OTM of 94.95%. Given the fundamentals of this market, the timing, and the premiums of these far OTM CALLs, sure points to an opportunity for some Time Farming!

The choices of which strikes to use for this trade, would depend on your confidence in the fundamental data, your risk tolerance, and your confidence in this type of trading. If you are new to this type of trading, please seriously consider doing paper-trading until you gain the confidence you need to pull-the-trigger. As you gain experience, you will probably have trades in more than one market, this also helps you spread your risks around and not have all your eggs in one basket. The matrix (below) date is June 2017, and the underlying is the SX7, NOV17 soybean contract.

	Open.Int	Prob.OT...	Last X	Bid X	Ask X	Exp	Strike	
NOV 17	(141)	1 /ZSX7					**CALL Options**	
	4,519	61.37%	35.875 G	36.750 G	37.250 G	/OZSX7	980	
	18,459	66.76%	31.625 G	31.500 G	31.875 G	/OZSX7	1000	
	5,029	71.35%	26.375 G	27.250 G	27.625 G	/OZSX7	1020	
	6,752	75.28%	23.125 G	23.625 G	24.000 G	/OZSX7	1040	
	5,918	78.55%	20.000 G	20.625 G	21.125 G	/OZSX7	1060	
	3,129	81.41%	18.250 G	18.250 G	18.625 G	/OZSX7	1080	
	34,275	83.73%	16.500 G	16.125 G	16.500 G	/OZSX7	1100	
	2,410	85.79%	14.500 G	14.375 G	14.750 G	/OZSX7	1120	
	4,993	87.49%	13.000 G	12.875 G	13.125 G	/OZSX7	1140	
	3,657	88.99%	11.000 G	11.500 G	11.875 G	/OZSX7	1160	
	1,968	90.25%	10.000 G	10.375 G	10.750 G	/OZSX7	1180	
	19,648	91.34%	9.000 G	9.375 G	9.750 G	/OZSX7	1200	
	800	92.28%	7.875 G	8.500 G	8.875 G	/OZSX7	1220	
	1,980	93.09%	7.125 G	7.750 G	8.000 G	/OZSX7	1240	
	1,637	93.78%	7.000 G	7.000 G	7.375 G	/OZSX7	1260	
	1,308	94.42%	6.500 G	6.500 G	6.750 G	/OZSX7	1280	
	10,117	94.95%	6.000 G	6.000 G	6.125 G	/OZSX7	1300	
	360	95.51%	5.250 G	5.375 G	5.625 G	/OZSX7	1320	
	582	95.91%	3.875 G	5.000 G	5.250 G	/OZSX7	1340	
	305	96.29%	3.375 G	4.500 G	4.750 G	/OZSX7	1360	
	243	96.64%	4.125 G	4.125 G	4.375 G	/OZSX7	1380	
	5,536	96.97%	3.875 G	3.875 G	4.000 G	/OZSX7	1400	**50% OTM**
	78	97.22%	3.500 G	3.500 G	3.750 G	/OZSX7	1420	
	259	97.52%	3.250 G	3.250 G	3.500 G	/OZSX7	1440	
	196	97.74%	3.000 G	3.000 G	3.250 G	/OZSX7	1460	
	292	97.89%	2.750 G	2.750 G	3.000 G	/OZSX7	1480	
	2,960	98.09%	2.500 G	2.500 G	2.750 G	/OZSX7	1500	

Now, use this same option matrix (NOV 2017 Soybean CALLs) and imagine we place a vertical credit bear spread by selling 10 of the 1300-strike CALLS while simultaneously buying 10 of the 1360 CALLS. It is likely we'd get a net credit of 1.50; in this example (see below) 1.50 for a credit. (1.50 X $50)= $75.00. Selling 10 of these spreads will result in a credit in the trading account (commissions not included) of $750.00. You can see from the matrix that the Prob. OTM for the 1300-strike CALL is 94.95%.

Spread	Side		Qty	Symbol		Exp	Strike	Type		Price	
VERTICAL	SELL		-10	/ZSX7 1/50 N...	/OZSX7	1300	CALL		1.50	LMT
	BUY		+10	/ZSX7 1/50 N...	/OZSX7	1360	CALL		CREDIT	

The initial margin requirement for this trade is $980 total. Remember, that is initial margin; you have to have reserves. This is another important thing you can learn to gauge by using the paper-trade mode of your trading platform; the amount of margin is automatically posted clearly each day for you to see. In this trade, the yield would be 750/980 = 76.5% in five months. You trading platform will tell you the exact margin requirement before you place a trade. The (1360 minus 1300) max risk and max margin would be 60 cents X $50= $3,000 per spread.

In this vertical credit spread, you keep all your credit so long as the 1300-strike option stays OTM. With soybeans near 916, the 1300-strike is about 40% OTM. There's plenty of "room" to exit the trade should the market fundamentals go adverse. For example, the 1300-strike CALL has a delta (not shown) of -0.08 and the 1360 long CALL has a delta of 0.06 (not shown). Together the net delta of the two options is only – 0.02. A 50-cent move up in prices would change the spread value by (50 x -.02) = -1.0 or   a loss of about -$50 per spread. (note: If you are not familiar with combining deltas: They are simply algebraically added to get the total delta for the option combination. There no requirement that you do these calculations in order to trade because your software will keep track of your trades P/L automatically.) Note: This paragraph was added for advanced option traders; these calculations are not required but only put here to confirm the math for experienced traders.

The advantages of using the vertical credit spread are: limited margin required, potential losses are limited instead of using a naked CALL where losses are theoretically unlimited. Conversely, the advantage of using a naked CALL is that you can write a strike farther OTM and collect more premium. You can see in the option matrix that the 1400-strike would net 3.875, and the 1500-strike would net 2.50, $193.75 and $125.00 respectively and their "Prob. OTM" is 96.97% (1400) and 98.09% (1500.)

Counter-Seasonal Profits

This example in counter-seasonal soybean trading illustrates how finding suitable trades can be done in any types of conditions (bear, bull, neutral) so long as we can determine a price bias and are able to sell strikes far enough OTM. In this soybean counter-seasonal market, we do not know how much a market may rebound, drop more, or stabilize; we only have fundamentals that offer us the view that *a bull market resurgence is extremely unlikely during a specific time period.*

Remember also that you are not strapped to selling only one strike, you can spread them out or mix them up as you please. If you are totally new to this type of trading, just keep it simple in the beginning. You must also realize that trading, even with a 98% probability of a win, does not mean you can just place a trade and not manage it. Sooner or later you will have a trade that takes a sudden and unexpected turn. We strive to place trades so far OTM with our short option strikes - that a moderate move against our position can be easily tolerated.

The commodity you are trading doesn't care one iota how much work you put into finding a trade, how good you are, or what you think. The markets are in no way personal, and they do what they do and you can't change it. Hope can be a very expensive emotion. The human brain is hard wired to find patterns in everything we see; this imagination is why we are at the top of the food chain but commodity trading is no place for any wishful thinking. While we use our imagination to consider what positions might make us money, using imagination to extend hope for a turnaround is most often a misplaced endeavor. Often, to be a successful trader, you must be ruthless in managing your trades. No one has a 100% success rate and keeping losses at acceptable limits is paramount to building your account.

Early Exits from Trades with Profits

One of the most useful tools you can develop in managing trades is to learn to keep your profits by limiting your risk exposure. Here's an example: A CALL is sold at a strike far OTM for a $500 premium; this hypothetical short CALL expires in 180 days. Suppose that after 100 days, the value of the short option has gone down to $150. This means if you continue to hold the trade, you are effectively risking your $350 profit for another 80 days to make the remaining $150. Clearly, the risk parameters of any trade can changed since we initialized the trade. Why might we wish to close this trade and simply take the nice $350 profit?

1. There could be a development in the market that has adverse potential.
2. Perhaps you have found other trades that have more potential than waiting out this one.
3. Psychologically, we perceive the $350 as a good win, and we just don't want to risk giving it, or a part of it back, just to make the remaining $150.

Whether or not you use #3 in the above list is a very interesting question. One person will love to take the profit and move on, while another might logically understand that she/he still has a 98% chance of keeping the remaining $150 and won't even consider exiting the trade. Strangely, the history of the trade up to the point in time of having to make this decision –will heavily influence a decision. If, in those first 100 days, you were up $400, then down to -$100, then back up to $350 – you will be more inclined to "take the $350 and move on." This is just "human nature."

On the other hand, if this trade has moved very smoothly in your favor at a slow but ample pace, you might be inclined to hold it a bit longer, so long as the fundamentals remain as they were when you placed the trade. In the end, because you are human, you will do what you want to do, then very perfectly rationalize your decision. Then after the remaining 80 days has passed, you can either:

1. Not look back. (highly recommended)
2. Feel very smart about your decision. ("Hero")
3. Or beat yourself up for making a "bad" choice. ("Goat")

Chapter 6 General Questions & Answers

Question: Which markets should I trade, and how many markets will I need to study?

Answer: Probably the worst thing a beginner can do is try to study too many markets. This commonly results in an analysis paralysis and mental fatigue. Proficiency at this trading is not proportional to the number of markets you can trade. The very first chapter in this book was "The Power of Mother Nature." Placing time-farming trades that harmonize with realistic seasonal price patterns are the best. For a beginner, the grain markets are a good choice. The units of contracts, the trading hours, and the seasonal price tendencies are all very similar, the margin requirements offer excellent leverage, and there is a plethora of information available on these markets along with well-researched USDA reports. Finding your favorite markets to trade is an individual decision. Obviously, markets that have strong seasonal tendencies and that you personally find interesting, are the best candidates for you. Trading far OTM options with high volume and ample open interests is best; these are both factors for availability, liquidity, and fair pricing. For those reasons, the smaller markets can often be eliminated.

Short answer: Pick 3 or 4 markets. If you don't find them interesting, drop one and add another. Don't spread yourself too thin; better to be knowledgeable at four markets than unsure about ten. If a market interests you, the first thing a new trader usually does is get the contract specifications, and begin to examine current and historical charts and price patterns, consult supply-demand data, look at historical pricing, and read market commentary from a reliable source.

Question: What's the best way to find trading ideas?

Answer: The answer to this question is quite simple. You already understand that you are looking for predictable price patterns, usually seasonal, and since you are Time Farming, you won't be trying to guess the exact timing or amplitude of price movements. What you seek is a market where the fundamentals clearly support a reliable price pattern; the more compelling the fundamentals of that market, the better. Remember to think in terms of price patterns over months of time; release any need you might feel to shoot for specific price targets (old stock trading habits die hard.) Seek out some sources with good commodity commentary. Begin to immerse yourself by reading commentary, following industry reports and/or USDA data, study price charts and price history of specific contracts of the commodity. You are looking for quality opportunities for profits over a period of months; it is not your goal to find a high number of trades. It can be a help to search for articles on seasonal tendencies in commodities, since that is a primary source for time-farming trades. Remember, unlike most traders, you are looking for reliable long-term price patterns, not quick price-targeting trades.

Question: What kind of broker will be best for me to use: Discount, Full-service, or Managed money?

Answer: There is no pat answer to this question. For self-directed smaller accounts, a discount broker with a great trading platform is probably best. If you enjoy studying the markets and learning about option strategies, you will likely use a discount online broker. On the other end of the spectrum, a sound experienced money manager can do all the work for you, if you have the funds to devote to a larger account. You must shop very carefully and be very mindful of the potential and the risks of this type of trading. If you are choosing a full-service broker, be sure and find out which commodity markets, if any, are their specialty. For example, a broker might specialize in handling trades in the grains, or energy markets. Many brokers allow smaller accounts, some don't, so ask about minimums as you choose a broker or brokers. If you are going to use a smaller self-directed account, be sure your broker provides free paper-trading mode, so you can practice using the platform and gain some mock experience before you put your money in real trades.

Not everyone is cutout to self direct their own trades; you could have time restrictions, or it could be that you just don't enjoy putting in the research work it takes to find trading opportunities. Chances are, if you don't enjoy this type of work, you won't be really good at it. Some people enjoy gardening and others hire a gardener; to each his/her own. If you have a substantial sum to trade and limited time to trade, drop me an email and I can offer some resources to consider. Just email me from my website at TimeFarming.com or send it to: Don@WriteThisDown.com

Question: Can I use the same seasonal trades every calendar year?

Answer: Yes and no. As a trader, what you may want to hear - is that there are never exceptions to hard and fast trading rules - but you know this just isn't true. *Knowing seasonal trends is only the first step; the fundamentals of a market must confirm that a seasonal trend is likely, or alternately, that a counter-seasonal trend is guiding the market.* You will develop lists of seasonal trends in commodity markets and you will visit the items on the list each and every year. Most often you will find semblance of the seasonal trend and even then, you must go to the fundamentals of that market for further confirmation. Most times the option strikes we sell are far enough OTM to weather some adversity from our market view. Still, such things as floods, prolonged droughts, political, regulatory, transportation disruptions, fuel prices, and other factors can influence the market we are trading. Many of these factors are unpredictable. To state the obvious, we must remain an alert and informed captain of each of our trades for its duration. Our work is not done when the trade is placed, diligence continues through the life of the trade.

Question: What does a "stronger dollar" (US$) mean for commodity prices?

Answer: There are dozens of courses and entire books dedicated to the subject of foreign exchange rates and policies. The answer supplied here will be simple and limited in scope. I will use a few examples:

The United States is the second largest exporter of soybeans (and soy products) in the world. When the US$ (US dollar) is "strong", this means that it takes more of a foreign currency to buy product; therefore, a "higher" or "stronger" dollar can mean the US product becomes more costly to buy in the international market and in turn this can cause a dip in demand causing prices to go down. Conversely, when the US$ is "down" or "weaker" compared to other currencies, US goods become cheaper overseas, demand increases and prices of the commodity can go up.

Commodity prices don't necessarily tick higher for every tick lower in the Dollar Index, but there is a strong inverse relationship over a long period of time. The fundamental supply and demand characteristics of commodity markets strongly move prices one way or another at times despite the direction of the U.S. currency. Exchange rates are only one of many factors.

Chapter 7 More Seasonal Trades

Cotton DEC Contract

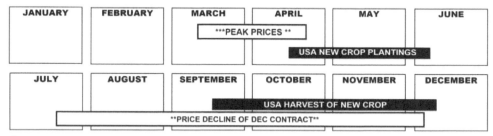

SEASONAL COTTON PRICES OF DEC CONTRACT

JANUARY	FEBRUARY	MARCH	APRIL	MAY	JUNE
		***PEAK PRICES **			
			USA NEW CROP PLANTINGS		

JULY	AUGUST	SEPTEMBER	OCTOBER	NOVEMBER	DECEMBER
		USA HARVEST OF NEW CROP			
	PRICE DECLINE OF DEC CONTRACT				

Current estimates for world cotton production are about 25 million tonnes or 110 million bales annually, accounting for 2.5% of the world's arable land. China is the world's largest producer of cotton, but most of this is used domestically. The United States is the world's 3rd largest producer behind India, and has been the largest exporter for many years. In the United States, cotton is usually measured in bales, which measure approximately 0.48 cubic meters (17 cubic feet) and weigh 226.8 kilograms (500 pounds). In the United States, planting is generally done by mid-June while harvesting runs from September to December, depending on geography. Price declines are usually a sell-off during August - October when harvesting is in full swing.

15 YEAR HISTORICAL AVERAGE SMOOTHED-LINE FOR DECEMBER COTTON CONTRACT

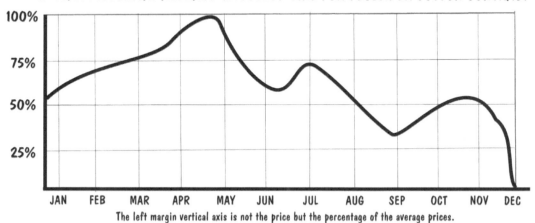

The left margin vertical axis is not the price but the percentage of the average prices.

Seasonal Trend
COTTON #2 DECEMBER 2017 CONTRACT ONE-YEAR

The DEC cotton contract in 2017 displayed a typical price pattern of the average of the last 15 years with prices peaking in N. American spring-summer months and declining into the second half of the calendar year. The strategy in this typical pattern is to sell far OTM DEC options, once the peak seasonal prices have topped. Of course, this must be confirmed by the cotton market's fundamental parameters, not by technical action. I would point out that this chart, like all price-history makes it look easy due to the "genius of hindsight". In reality, before prices fully confirm a seasonal turn, a trader might wait a couple of months into the growing season to place the (far OTM short CALL option) trades. This wait allows time for the "in-the-ground" crops to develop more fully (production becomes less risky.) The monthly USDA crop reports will confirm the progress of the new crop, demand, yield projections, and other factors that may confirm expected price trends.

The 15-year *smoothed-line historical price chart* (Seasonal Cotton Prices of DEC Contract) indicates what appears to be a sharp drop-off in NOV into DEC. To neophyte traders, this may look like an opportunity to hold off to late in the season to place a trade, but this is problematic for a couple of reasons: First, waiting to make a short 30-day window trade is very risky. The time value of the option premium is much smaller due to the very short time until expiration, and frankly, 15-year (or longer histories) charts can be deceiving in that while they display a big picture, they are less accurate in locating short-timed trades. Ideally, time-farming type trades want high option premiums by selling into long-term price moves, while also collecting lots of time premium over months not just two to four weeks of time premium decay. It can be a big error to "zero in" on minor price variations with long-term history charts. I'm repeating an earlier suggestion here, but if you have the chart resources, print the last ten or 15 years of individual contracts charts – and you will see the proof of how often the actual price variance (timing) will differ from a 15-year history average plot. Multi-year average price charts are not for short-term trading (ever!)

I would caution you against bringing what I will call "stock trading habits" into your commodity trading. Remember most ag commodities are annuals; new plantings happen each year, plus climatological conditions often make or break a crop year without notice. Agricultural commodity trading is both science and art, the fundamentals of these markets can quickly swamp technical trading techniques you import from your stock market trading.

Soybeans July Contract

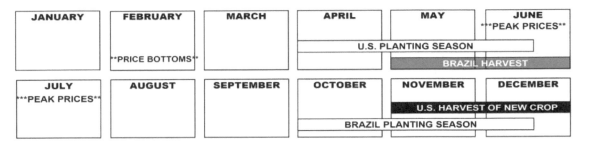

The soybean market is dominated by two major producers: Brazil and the United States. Soybeans are harvested in November-December in the U.S., while the Brazil harvest takes place in May-June. Most of the U.S. crop is sold soon after harvest, driving prices down. Some of the crop is held until spring, hoping for better prices. US farmers need to raise cash for the spring planting and to make storage room for new crop. So in mid/late winter the remainder of stock are sold and the annual low prices occur, often in February. The Brazilian harvest will not reach the markets until June-July.

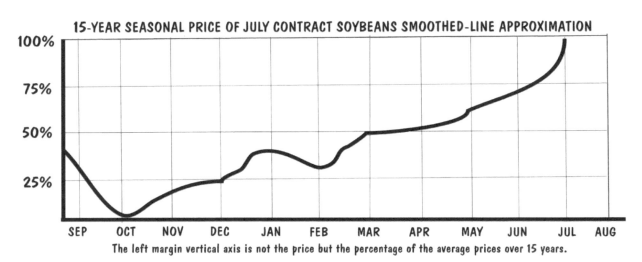

The left margin vertical axis is not the price but the percentage of the average prices over 15 years.

As you can see from the graphic, the price of Soybean JUL contract normally rises in the first half of the calendar year. Being aware of this seasonal trend is only a starting place; I am saying it would be reckless of you just to buy the JUL soybean contract in JAN based only on the 15- year history of prices without doing any further research.

The primary reason this is only a *starting place*, has everything to do with economics 101: supply and demand. For example if soybean prices have been high, very often farmers will plant them knowing that stocks have been low as they anticipate profits for the new crop (the new season's crop, the crop farmers will plant next.) The USDA in their monthly reports anticipate how many acres of a crop will be planted (based on survey information). They also estimate the yield (how many bushels per acre). From this the total yield of the new crop will be estimated, then the amount of soybeans in stock (storage) will be added to the anticipated new crop. Next, demand will be estimated; this includes both domestic use and the amount of exports. Then, consumption (demand) is subtracted from stocks + new crop, and the "end of crop year" stocks are estimated (often just called "ending stocks".) This calculation (still an estimate) will be compared to consumption (demand) to arrive at a stocks-to-use (STU) ratio.

At this point an investor or a producer (farmer) will compare this estimated STU (expressed as a percentage) to a price history versus previous year's STU to try and gauge a trading range for the new crop prices. If, for example, the STU for a new crop is at the highest it's been for the last five years AND current supplies (stocks) are more than ample, there could be a bearish outlook for prices. Conversely, if stocks and STU are low and trending lower, this might be a bullish outlook for prices.

Now in plain language: If production will far exceed the amount needed, prices go down. If there isn't enough stored and grown to keep up with usage, prices will go up. Voila! Supply and Demand. The STU (stocks-to-use ratio) is the closet thing we have to a "one number" snapshot of classic supply-demand.

The USDA issues crop reports every month. Due to seasonal cycles of planting and harvest, some specific monthly reports (depending on the crop) will be much more important than others. In the case of soybeans, the other major producer (Brazil) has a southern hemisphere season that mirrors the northern hemisphere seasons. For this reason, the world supply – and therefore prices – are influenced by crops in top producing regions. The top five world producers of soybeans are US, Brazil, Argentina, China, and India.

There is a division of the USDA call the ERS, Economic Research Service. The URL to link on the web is: https://www.ers.usda.gov

There you can call up information per crop name and find almost any stats you can imagine. I would say this web site should be a first-stop to your researching any commodity you are considering trading.

There are scores of major universities in farming regions that provide data and research on many different crops. For example University of Illinois for corn, soybeans, and more is at:

http://farmdocdaily.illinois.edu/newcategories/marketing_and_outlook/crop_yields/

You can also Google to find podcast, blogs, and video/audio crop reports and commentary.

Chapter 8 Time Farming Trade Psychology

Time Farming can be a way for you to exit the "trader's roller coaster." The illustration below has been around for years in it's various forms and every experienced trader is probably too familiar with it.

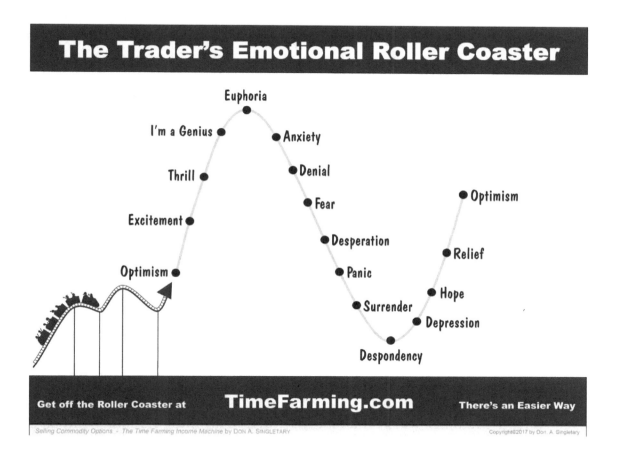

A little base anxiety about a trade might be a good thing; it prevents us from becoming complacent but this doesn't mean we should go through a roller-coaster ride of emotions. By re-setting the way we go about setting up and executing trades, we define both our expectations and the emotions we experience in managing trades. There is the old dilemma of a fellow who was in a train tunnel and his immediate problem became: Was it the "light at the end of the tunnel" he saw or the headlight of an on-coming train? My own reaction to this problem is to immediately ask, "What the hell was he doing in the tunnel in the first place?"

If during a trade you have asked yourself the same question, then you may appreciate this new way to trade. I am going to ask you to indulge me with my train analogies for a just a moment longer:

If you are walking a train track and you look up and suddenly see and hear a train at full speed only fifty yards away, you panic! But if you see it coming down the track and it's still a mile away, you still have plenty of time to get out of it's way. This would allow you to simply and calmly step aside – and you remain unemotional and safe. If you are Time Farming correctly, you should never have to panic. The options you sell should be months out in the future and the strike prices you select should be very far OTM (out of the money.)

There is a time mindset in writing far OTM options in ag commodities. Just as a corn or cotton farmer knows that a crop is not made in a few days or even a few weeks, this type of trading is based on a long-term view. Most of your trades will span several months of time. This perspective is new to many traders. Managing these Time Farming trades is more a practice of tracking the fundamentals of a market, rather than constantly consulting daily price fluctuations. As time nears an option's expiration date, the *more certain* we should become that we have a successful trade. This is almost the exact opposite of conventional trading that often involves price-targeting methods that are time critical.

We maintained from the beginning of this book that you could use the same math that insurance companies and casinos use to amass profits. You don't see the casino manager panicking every time a customer wins on a slot machine, or winning hands at the blackjack table, and neither should you be bothered when you must exit a trade, so long as you are managing your trades responsibly. Insurance companies pay thousands of claims every day and yet they are among the most profitable types of all businesses. With the Time Farming method of trading, over time you should be placing trades that make you more like the owner of your own casino than the gambler who enters it. If not, rethink what you are doing.

Three or Four Markets Is All You Need

If you can follow and learn as few as three or four commodity markets, you have a real chance at doing rather well with your trading. Where stock trading will often involve following scores of equities, an individual's commodity trading is usually limited to about four to six markets or less. While the DOW and S&P indices can be described as the "tide that raises and lowers all boats," commodity markets have very specific and individual characteristics (although commodity groups like grains often move in sympathy.) Commodity research is about the *depth* of your research, not about how many markets you can learn to follow. So what exactly does *depth of research* mean? It means developing trusted sources and reliable data on the markets you choose to trade. The US Government spends hundreds of millions of dollars in ag research and tracking crop economical research and they have a lot of very talented and experienced people who do the work. USDA reports play a vital role in tracking supply-demand, stored stocks of food and energy, and also reporting from scores of countries around the world. The information in the free monthly USDA crop reports is a staple in commodity trading.

As you begin to follow specific markets, you will also see many reports from universities located in prime agricultural belts. Most of these universities offer free emailed reports of one or more crops. There are also research services, such as The Hightower Report, Moore Research Center, CRG (Commodity Research Group), and many more. It is quite usual to find companies and/or blogs that specialize in specific commodities.

Chapter 9 The Other Side of the Commodity Markets

I spent almost 25 years as a private commodity risk management consultant. My customers were either producers of commodities or purchasers of commodities. As you trade and read more about commodity trading you will hear the term "the commercials." This is a term that means the large producers and buyers of commodities, the companies in the business side of the market positions. You should know that these commercial accounts that trade commodities and futures are on *both sides* of the market. Both sides of the commercial markets are hedgers; they use futures and options on futures to help control risk exposure to price changes and delivery risks. An orange juice plant or orange grower will lock in high prices to protect profit margins. A large grocery store chain that buy millions of dollars worth of orange juice will lock in low prices to protect profit margins. By balancing either production or purchasing requirements, businesses use futures trading to mitigate risk and preserve margins. This doesn't mean they are any more certain about predicting prices than you are; they just use the futures market to sell the risks to traders on respective sides of the market. A commercial account trades futures to mitigate risks; the speculator trades futures to make money; either the commercials or speculators can trade on either side of the market (being either *buyers* or *sellers*.) The result of all these trading transactions is that offer balance to prices over time; this is the primary purpose of the futures and commodity markets. This balance, over time, keeps the prices of commodities reasonable according to actual supply and demand factors, and prices are generally not subject to wild fluctuations. In plain language: this is what keeps us from having a bag of flour, a loaf of bread or a gallon of orange juice or gasoline from having a price that fluctuates wildly from one week to the next.

A trucking company would not be able to promise a customer a fixed price for a long period of time unless they are able to use futures to "lock in" their purchase price of fuel. Companies that make and sell clothing from cotton have to protect themselves from having to pay high prices for raw material; they wouldn't be able to promise people who sell their goods fixed prices. Cattle farmers would be subject to wild fluctuations in feed prices if they could not "forward purchase" feed for their stocks, and could be put out of business by high corn prices if it were not for the futures markets. Roughly 40% of corn production is used for ethanol production and 36% is used for animal feed. Most gasoline sold in the US is up to ten percent ethanol.

Why Time Farming is Relatively New

Not too many years ago, the average investor did not invest in commodities because doing so required significant amounts of time, money and expertise. Today, there are many different routes to the commodity markets for the non-professional traders to participate. Free software, free quotes, deeply discounted commissions, and modern computers and mobile devices have leveled the playing field. Prior to the early 1990's, ag options on commodity futures were virtually non-existent, and a simple business or home setup with quote machines and the fees paid for live quotes would typically cost a few thousand dollars per month – and even then, trades were primarily handled by live telephone interaction with a broker.

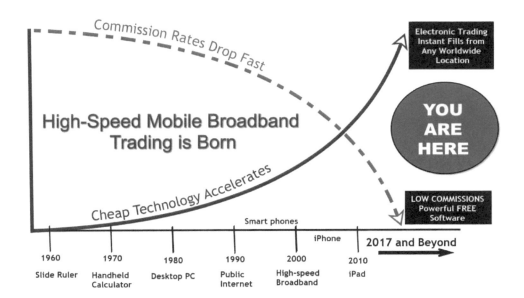

The Learning Curve

Every attempt has been made in this book to make the information on Time Farming strategies as clear and transparent as possible. Still, there are a lot of readers that have no experience in either trading options or trading futures (commodity) contracts. For those, your entry into futures trading can be made easier by the CME links in Chapter One. If you are new to options trading, try not to be overwhelmed. There are only two option-trading strategies to learn: writing (selling CALLs) and the vertical credit spreads (bull and bear).

Remember to send for the free "Time Farming PDF" file by emailing me at: Don@WriteThisDown.com and putting TIME FARMING in the subject line. This PDF file has some links to basic option theory and also some links to help you learn more about USDA reports (free subscriptions to their reports), and a few links that can help you learn more about the fundamentals of some of the commodity markets.

If you have only limited experience and you want to accelerate your learning curve on how to find and manage Time Farming trades, I have created an educational service where you can get monthly information on specific trades using real-time trades and money management. It is a paid service call the **Time-Farming Newsletter:** *Monthly Training Bulletins.* It is only natural that anyone with limited experience with futures and the options trading should be cautious about placing your first trades. All of us need a level of confidence in order to pull-the-trigger. This service is available at our web site: http://www.TimeFarming.com

Rarely does one learn everything about a new trading method by just reading a book. After understanding the basics, there is a time period for trying and testing ideas. This newsletter can help you speed up the process of gaining the knowledge and confidence you'll need to pull the trigger on Time Farming trades.

Here's what the MONTHLY TRAINING BULLETIN contains:

- Full commentary on at least two trades and strategies each month.
- Supply-Demand Research with commentary on real time trade illustrations.
- Price charts and historical 15-year seasonal price trends of each commodity contract illustrated.

- Free access to our Selling Commodity Options Articles.
- Each monthly has Q&A (Questions & Answers) of frequently ask questions (FAQ's)
- You will also receive bulletins at any time (same day) as trades are cancelled, closed, or modified in any way – so you can follow along in real-time.

I highly recommend you use your online broker's practice (paper-tradeing) account to enter these trades and follow along in real time. This will give great information, experience, analytics, and insight as to how to find and place trades. This is not a trade advisory service; it is for educational purposes only.

There is presently a large discount on a three-month trial subscription for people who have bought this book. For more information go to TimeFarming.com There is a link there where you can send me any questions you may have about the MONTHLY TRAINING BULLETIN newsletter. My hope is that it can help you save time and money and learn to trade with confidence. If you already know options and commodity trading, you have a great head start to some very unique and profitable trading.

If you are lucky enough to have more money than time, and would rather have someone manage your money, contact me and I can send you information on some services outside my offices.   I do not manage other people's money, nor am I a trade advisor or broker.

Remember to sign-up for my free PDF with some tips and links to resources by sending an email to me at: Don@WriteThisDown.com Put TIME FARMING in the subject line please. Thank you and good luck. I am a professional writer and I enjoy helping people along; this is why I created the MONTHLY TRAINING BULLETIN newsletter. I do think it will make learning more about Time Farming more interesting, easier and faster for you.

Chapter 10 Expert Level: Tips for Advanced Option Traders

While utilizing Time-Farming strategies requires a knowledge of option basics, there are many traders with advanced experience and option knowledge that are just now being introduced to this type of trading. This messages here are written with more experienced option traders in mind.

Ratio Credit Spreads

A ratio credit spread is an ingenious way of limiting margin requirements should the underlying make adverse price moves to your strategy. The *ratio credit spread* is usually selling two or more options far out-of-the-money options while simultaneously buying an option closer to the money for a net credit. This strategy can offer more potential profit on a trade while offering protection by limiting the draw-down. To refresh your ideas on how to employ this method, the pros at OptionsSellers.com offer several articles with great comments at their blog. see: https://www.optionsellers.com/?s=ratio+credit+spread Michael Gross and James Cordier, who manage money and accounts for high-end investors use this strategy often and have written many good articles on its use.

On Implied Volatility

Experienced option traders are very keen on how to use implied volatility (IV%) when trading options. When selling options, the goal is to sell high IV% and conversely, in buying options purchasing low or lower IV% options is desirable. In Time Farming trades we often sell options at 60 to 90 days out and more. Due to the long time frame of these trades, it is quite common for IV% to cycle through highs and/or lows. Of course it is always the preference to have IV% aid a trade, but since many trades are for months of time – the trader can experience ebbs and flows of IV% over these extended times. IV% is always important in option trading although trades held for months cannot always ride the tide of volatility.

Having said that, a trader can always add to a position when volatility spikes present the opportunity – while the fundamentals still support current positions.

Strangles

Most of the text in this book addresses trades in harmony with commodity seasonal price trends whether they be in sync with historical price patterns or placed during undeniable counter-seasonal price patterns. However, there are opportunities when the trader thinks a market's fundamentals strongly warrant adherence to a *price range* over a period of time. The *short strangle* strategy is ideal for this market view. Simultaneously selling far OTM CALLS and PUTS for a credit, can offer more bang for the buck by requiring less margin money. If these trades can be placed during high IV% spikes, this is even better. For advanced traders there may be an opportunity to place mirrored vertical credit spreads above and below the trading range for a *butterfly*. Turning a short naked option into a vertical credit spread is possible by "legging in" to the additional option(s) is a possibility. Or using price swings as an opportunity to convert a naked option into a wide strangle is also a possibility. While I don't recommend these ideas for beginners, experienced traders often have an ability to improve a trade with one or more of these strategies. Some of these strategies offer opportunities for improved money management that can free up capital for other positions.

How Far OTM?

One of the most common questions about selling options is "How far out-of-the-money should I go?" The short answer is: As far as possible! Selling options 30%, 40%, even 50% OTM can be quite common. Experienced traders of commodities grow to understand the price behavior of selected commodities over years of time and a lot of experience makes it much easier to find and recognize seasonal and counter-seasonal price swings. While stock traders may be more focused on a quarterly earnings report, commodity traders typically use a much broader time stroke when assessing price movements (or lack thereof.) Even the most experienced stock option traders cannot so automatically transfer their experience to commodity markets. "How far OTM?" really depends on the typical price moves of individual commodities; I'm saying that the answer will depend on the market(s) you are trading.

The advantage of having a full-time manager with years of following these markets place trades on your behalf is attractive. Having said that, unless you have fund allocations of $250,000 and up for this type of trading, you probably may not qualify for this type of account. If you have that type of money, you can probably afford to have a qualified professional do the trades for you. If that's the case, this book will provide you with a good understanding of the trading strategies.

Most people who read this book will handle their own accounts, and will rely on investing their time and efforts to mine good trades. If you are one of these, and you use a deep-discount online broker, you have the advantage of extremely low commissions. These very low commissions will allow you to use farther OTM strikes; this can be a huge advantage as this will increase the mathematical odds of success.

Time Farming is a relatively sophisticated strategy. It takes time and effort to be successful at it. To help make it easier and save time for self-directed investors, I have developed the Time Farming newsletter: *Monthly Training Bulletin*, subscriptions are available at TimeFarming.com Even though Time Farming, when done correctly, doesn't require you live with your nose glued to the computer screen, I would never term this type trading as "set it and forget it."

If you do have $250,000 or more to allocate to this type of trading, contact me and I can refer you to a qualified money manager to help you invest. I always welcome comments and questions from readers to help me improve my books and articles. I can't always reply quickly but please just email at this address: Don@WriteThisDown.com   Thank you and good trading.

Other books by the author – all available on Amazon Bookstore

If you need to learn option trading, consider *Options Exposed Playbook,* a solid introduction to trading options with over 20 top strategies illustrated and explained in plain language. This book has been used by thousands of option traders and it is known for its easy-to-read introduction to options.

The Amazing Covered Call – Triple Income Made Easy
If you own a portfolio of stocks in a regular or retirement account, you could be leaving money on the table. This common and conservative strategy can make an additional 6% to %15 per year and could shorten your road to retirement!

Almost everywhere I go, I always hear people say, "I need to learn about stocks." So I wrote a book for the person who knows little-to-nothing about the stock market, can spend less than two hours with - and they will have the knowledge and understanding to confidently invest in stocks. Grandparents have bought copies for all their grandkids and this book is being used in several high schools and colleges to teach financial literacy. I'm especially proud to offer this book for those who want an entry level fun start to personal investing. Contact me for bulk buys for schools at a price discount.

Thank you for your support and good trading to you.
  – Don A. Singletary

Made in United States
Troutdale, OR
09/22/2023

13121619R00046